The Fireside Book

A picture and a poem
for every mood
chosen by

David Hope

Printed and published by
D.C. THOMSON & CO., LTD.,
185 Fleet Street, LONDON EC4A 2HS.
© D.C. Thomson & Co., Ltd., 2003.
ISBN 0-85116-833-7

APRIL

S	M	T	W	T	F	S
				1	2	3
4	5	6	7	8	9	10
11	12	13	14	15	16	17
18	19	20	21	22	23	24
25	26	27	28	29	30	

MAY

S	M	T	W	T	F	S
						1
2	3	4	5	6	7	8
9	10	11	12	13	14	15
16	17	18	19	20	21	22
23	24	25	26	27	28	29
30	31					

JUNE

S	M	T	W	T	F	S
		1	2	3	4	5
6	7	8	9	10	11	12
13	14	15	16	17	18	19
20	21	22	23	24	25	26
27	28	29	30			

CONTENTS

JANUARY CONTRAST

THE wind is whistling through the house
And rattling at the pane,
For Winter with its icy blast
Is here with sleet and rain.
It all seems grey and bleak without
No gleam to pierce the gloom,
It's quite a contrast from within
My warm and cosy room.

For there the fire in the hearth
Gives out a cheery blaze,
Dispelling all the cold and damp
Of January days.
There are some books and needlepoint,
A tray with pot of tea,
My tabby cat curled on the mat
Is dozing lazily.

As darkness falls, the curtains pulled
Drawn closed against the night,
And lamps that shed their steady glow
Are burning clear and bright.
The world within my little room
Feels cosy and secure —
Let January do her worst
Outside the big front door.

Kathleen Gillum

WINTER SONNET

NOW Summer blood dries golden; laced along
  The shivering air and through the jittery trees
A cold red flame is licking down a throng,
A crackling harvest of deep-tinted leaves.
Now Winter glowers in the sky where no
Heyday of blue is splashed among the cream-
Cheeked clouds: like phantom butterflies the snow
Falls feathery and specks the darkling stream.

But do not think that Winter is the end's
Beginning or that snow can seal for good,
For Spring's night-watchman rubs his hands and tends
The braziers of life: near the white wood
A seed is crouching, waiting for the sign
And coils of birth are ready to unwind.

R.L. Cook

SNOW

OUT of the bosom of the air,
  Out of the cloudfolds of her garment shaken,
Over the woodlands, brown and bare,
Over the harvest-fields forsaken,
Silent, and soft, and slow
Descends the snow.

Henry Wadsworth Longfellow

SNOWDROPS

THE fairy firstlings of the year
   Break through on Winter's scene,
Dainty, fragile bells of white
On slender stalks of green.
They seem to spring up overnight
Amidst the snow and hail,
So aptly named, a drop of snow
So delicate and frail.
Just at the very sight of them
My heart begins to sing,
For they proclaim in Wintertime
The promise of the Spring.

Kathleen Gillum

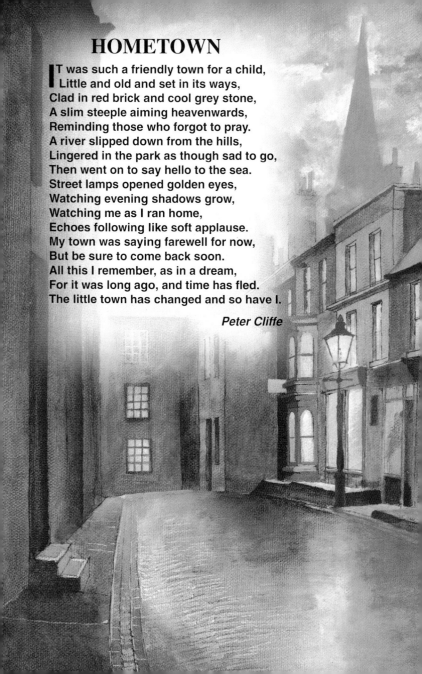

HOMETOWN

IT was such a friendly town for a child,
Little and old and set in its ways,
Clad in red brick and cool grey stone,
A slim steeple aiming heavenwards,
Reminding those who forgot to pray.
A river slipped down from the hills,
Lingered in the park as though sad to go,
Then went on to say hello to the sea.
Street lamps opened golden eyes,
Watching evening shadows grow,
Watching me as I ran home,
Echoes following like soft applause.
My town was saying farewell for now,
But be sure to come back soon.
All this I remember, as in a dream,
For it was long ago, and time has fled.
The little town has changed and so have I.

Peter Cliffe

RIVER DEE

BETWEEN the heathered hills, fair Dee,
Your ripples seem to pace
Like horses trotting o'er a lea,
With elegance and grace.

You brush sequestered, daisy banks
Where timid, thirsty deer
Wander on nimble, slender shanks,
To drink sweet waters clear.

A lovely river of renown
You freely forge ahead,
Washing primeval, jagged stone
Lain on a granite bed.

Beautiful feature of a realm
That's steeped in history,
You never fail to overwhelm
The hearts of spirits free.

Alice Jean Don

LAURENCEKIRK

THE lapwings are back in the low sky
    Across the crumbled fields of Spring
As a torn sun glitters the new-ploughed earth
And snowflake gulls flurry behind the tractor's lurch.
Scotland is coming bleary from her sleep;
Like a mother that's given birth, weary,
Her eyes are slowly coming round, unclouding,
As rain scorns a hill there, and braids of rainbow
Celebrate the greyness of the far North Sea.
But always, always, the lapwings tumble in the
    bright new fields
And now, as always, I don't know
Whether they laugh or weep.

Kenneth C. Steven

THE HARBOUR

THE morning light streams
    radiant beams
Across the sparkling sea,
And falls upon the bobbing boats
Moored safely by the quay.
Fishing vessels, cabin cruisers
Yachts of every size,
Tall masts and riggings, snowy sails
Stand out against blue skies.

There's seaweed tangled in old ropes
Of crafts that creak and sway,
And in the air and on my lips
Is tang of salty spray.
Fishing nets and lobster pots
The gulls that wheel and cry,
Are all part of the harbour life
To casual passers-by.

The gentle lapping of the waves
Against the old sea wall,
Is echoing the rhythmic sound
Of tides that ebb and fall.
And in the evening twinkling lights
Reflect across the bay,
As dusk falls on the harbour
At the ending of the day.

Kathleen Gillum

PEACEFUL WATERS

BENEATH a gently waning sun,
 Set in a silvery sky,
Two swans upon a limpid lake
Float so serenely by.

Life-long companions, we are told,
How gracefully they glide,
Two birds, with faithful, loving hearts,
For ever side by side.

Upon the bank, the trailing boughs
Of willow whisper low
As, through their pale green tapestry,
The little breezes blow.

And all the evening's hushed and still,
Save for soft murmurings,
And two white swans, inseparable,
With silver-dappled wings.

In harmony with nature's mood,
With every trembling star,
I wonder — do they realise
How beautiful they are?

Kathleen O'Farrell

SANDSTONE SPLENDOUR

GAUNT mountains, wild and free,
   What splendour to the fretted west you bring,
All quartzite-crowned, your corries echoing
The heartbeat of the sea.

And when the light is gone,
And day folds like the petals of a flower,
In moth-grey dusk, or silent, starlit hour
Your magic lingers on.

Pale shadows on the blue,
Like spectral towers your terraced summits rise,
Moon-washed and strange beneath the jewelled skies,
Their beauty born anew.

Proud hills in sun or rain,
Older than Eden, changeless in your peace,
What is your secret, that you never cease
To call us back again?

Brenda G. Macrow

THEN

WE rattled and thumped across Mull, baggage
and boxes and talk
In the beginning of April. Springtime was coming alive,
Creeping up through the cracks in the rocks
In daffodils, like the bright waving of children.
Now the skies glowered like the devil, rain clattered
Black and glassy over the windscreen, huge winds
Lifted hills into mist and dragoned the waves to silver.
In the middle of water, caught between greens and blues
Between jags of rocks, an otter showed off
In a playground of impossible somersaults, and vanished.
Then, out of the dark heart of the thunderheads,
Down at the end of the island where the Atlantic truly begins,
A blessing of light showered from an invisible hand
Turned golden the ocean in a Midas touch,
That single moment of our lives.

Kenneth C. Steven

LILIES OF THE VALLEY

NOW, at last, dear April's here,
Heralding the time of year
When flowers bloom and blackbirds sing,
To tell us, once again, it's Spring,
Wild daffodils, anemones,
In random drifts beneath the trees,
Magnolia's creamy velvet flowers,
Refreshed by sudden Springtime showers,
Flowers, flowers everywhere,
Compelling us to stand and stare,
But, of all the ones we meet,
How could they ever be as sweet,
As when the lilies of the valley,
Softly, as a sunrise, sally.

Brian Hope Gent

EVENING

A STILLNESS and a silence seal this
Hour, fragrant with May,
While dusk, night's gentle runner, comes and
Sponges light away.

Dim scented pools of day float, fading,
Under bird-tongued trees:
In their green depths light lies, reflecting
Sad symphonic seas.

Now nature rests and smoky darkness
Laces purple frills
Along the road that leads to nightfall
In the velvet hills.

R.L. Cook

LONG-TAILED TITS, MALVERN

COMPOSED outside my window
A group of crotchet tails
Stretched and straight
With minim heads
Pausing on the fir branch
Playing an Elgar score
Until — in six-eight time
They fly
And the music
Is no more.

David Elder

DAYS OF SUNSHINE

To sally in the brighter green
  And over mountains high
To glimpse the rays of dappled sun
The splendour in the sky.
There's music in each happy hour
Of dew upon the grass
The swish of silver birches
Nudging oak and elm and ash.
And on the sweeter fragrance
Cupped in the leafy glade
Enchantment washing over
Bonny bluebells in the shade.
Suddenly in gossamer
A butterfly flits the bough
Settling in the tulip bed
World in bloom resplendent now.

Dorothy McGregor

IONA

A GNARLED rock
Washed in the sea so long
All but the bone is gone.

Rattled year after year
In the mouth of the wind
Till the land is bare and naked.

Is it the prayers
That raise orchids every Spring
White and mauve from the granite?

Is it an ancient love
That brings the skylarks on strings of song
From this thin and brittle moorland?

Is it the very breath of heaven
That wakes sunlight here
Through the long gold of Summer?

Kenneth C. Steven

BUTTERFLY

OH butterfly so full of grace,
  How you flit from place to place;
No matter you are not exotic
Nor come from some far distant tropic,
Your magic lies within your wings
Which love the warmth that Summer brings;
Those wings as white as Winter snow,
Bring us joy where 'ere you go,
However could you come to this,
Born of a wrinkled chrysalis;
No, you must come from fairyland
With a wand held in your hand;
Such beauty makes our day seem bright
So thank you mistress "Cabbage White"!

Brian Hope Gent

NATURE'S COLOURS

SCARLET poppies 'midst golden corn
Pinkish tinge at the flush of dawn,
Clouds of alabaster white
Midnight blue of the depth of night,
Turquoise sheen on a dragonfly
Shades of grey in a stormy sky.

Buttercups on a bank of green
Opal ripples in a stream,
Amber honey in a jar
Silver light from a twinkling star,
A yellow daisy in a bowl
Inky black of a piece of coal.

Pearl of moonlight on the snow
Rosy hue of the sunset glow,
In cool brown earth drenched with the dew
And vivid flowers of every hue,
In blossom, bird and butterfly
Are colours which delight the eye.

Kathleen Gillum

MY FRIENDLY HILL

MY FRIENDLY hill with wildlife teems,
Above the meadows and the streams;
Its features are caressed by mist,
And by the rain so freely kissed.

Upon the heather's purple hue
Are sparkling diamonds of dew,
Precious jewels that catch my eye,
The gems that money cannot buy.

There, clinging to the mountainside,
A white-washed farm contrives to hide;
While here, an ancient church of stone,
With tombstones old but few to mourn.

Green glades abound and quiet dells,
With reservoirs where water swells
From the gushing, crystal-clear brooks,
Past leafy lanes and shady nooks.

Across this hill I used to stride
To view the countryside with pride —
The landscape of my native heath
Spread out before me far beneath.

My friendly hill, where I was born,
O'er which I roamed at night and morn,
When long forgotten is my name,
You will remain through time the same.

Glynfab John

HARLEQUIN AND COLUMBINE

OUR love is young, it is divine:
A joyous song, a sparkling wine,
For I am yours and you are mine,
Said Harlequin to Columbine.

When middle years around us twine,
Let love and trust our lives combine,
While o'er our heads the sun will shine,
Said Harlequin to Columbine.

When love grows old, shall we repine,
Or seek to read God's great design?
No! I'll be yours and you still mine,
Said Harlequin to Columbine.

Peter Cliffe

THE GRASSHOPPER
AND THE CRICKET

THE poetry of earth is never dead:
  When all the birds are faint with the hot sun,
And hide in cooling trees, a voice will run
From hedge to hedge about the new-mown mead:
This is the grasshopper's — he takes the lead
In Summer luxury — he has never done
With his delights, for when tired out with fun,
He rests at ease beneath some pleasant weed.

The poetry of earth is ceasing never:
On a lone Winter evening, when the frost
Has wrought a silence, from the stove there shrills,
The Cricket's song, in warmth increasing ever,
And seems to one in drowsiness half lost,
The grasshopper's among the grassy hills.

John Keats

COFFEE MORNING

CLIMBING in digestive hills,
where teeth-marked ridges
nibble at a biscuit-tin sky,
giants dunk boulders in streams of espresso
that swirl their cappuccino froth
beside the forgotten porcelain
of old bones.
Far below, silver foil lochs
reflect crumbs of islands
until carelessly crumpled
by a chattering wind.

Rowena M. Love

MY LOVELY JENNY

THE sun first rising in the morn,
   That tips the dew-bespangled thorn,
Does not so much the day adorn,
As does my lovely Jenny.

The zephyr's air the violet blows,
Or breathes upon the damask rose,
Does not half the beauty disclose
That does my lovely Jenny.

I stole a kiss the other day,
Believe me, naught but truth I say,
The fragrant breath of blooming May
Was not so sweet as Jenny.

Were she arrayed in rustic weed,
With her the bleating flocks I'd feed,
And call them with my piping reed,
To please my lovely Jenny.

And when in slumber's lap of rest,
He streaks with gold the ruddy west,
He's not so beautiful at best,
As is my lovely Jenny.

While bees from flower to flower still fly,
And linnets warble through the sky,
Or stately swans the waters ply,
So long shall I love Jenny.

Glynfab John

A FRIEND'S GARDEN

WARM as an outstretched hand, a verdant place,
Wearing 'a sweet disorder in the dress'.
Heavy with blossom lovingly allowed
To hang in rich, unbridled fruitfulness.
No close-clipped hedges here, or shaven lawns
To mutely disapprove of carefree tread,
But drifts of daisy stars, soft clouds of broom
And clustered boughs embracing overhead.
Forgotten blooms that graced the long ago
Hold court with tremulous first-season flowers.
No growing thing too poor to mingle here
And cast its scent upon the shadow-hours
When leaves and grass and branches gently merge
Into the gauzy veils of Summer night,
Where homing birds and small, soft-footed things
Move secretly among the fading light.

Joan Howes

WONDERS

BIRDSONG and windsong
  Dewdrops at dawn
A carpet of sparkles
Laid out on the lawn.
Petals and pollen
And striped fluffy bees
Visiting flowers
And blossoms on trees.

Starlight and moonlight
Shine down from on high
The splendour of sunrise
That flushes the sky.
Frost on the trellis
All glittering bright
Feathers of snowflakes
That drift through the night.

Rain clouds and rainbows
And sunflowers of gold
Poppies of scarlet
That blaze bright and bold.
Nature brings beauty
In which we can share
For all of her wonders
Abound everywhere.

Kathleen Gillum

NIGHTLY NOCTURNES

THE Milky Way arcs in the sky,
　As zephyr breezes gently sigh,
Bats and owls have taken flight,
To start their vigil of the night,
Flower petals gently close,
Folding to a sweet repose,
Sleeping creatures small and large,
Complete the countryside's montage,
And so the twilight cavalcade,
Takes place in every leafy glade,
Nightly nature's nocturnes play,
In homage to the coming day.

Brian Hope Gent

SEASCAPE
(BORGH BEACH, BARRA)

ALL shimmering bright, this island paradise
Jewels the skyline of the Summer day
Pinned to a radiant, rainbow-hued array
Of rippling satin called the sea,
As though once laid aside by Nature's hand
Carefully in a scarce-frequented nook
Of this her orb; fashioned in true likeness
Of her sketches; textured to display
Her matchless skill;
But torn in second thought from out her book;
Too rich and glorious for everyday.
This is no palm-fringed coral shore.
Reflections in the silver-sequinned rocks
And subtle sounds merged in the breakers' roar;
The homely bleating of the machair flocks
And peat-smoke drifting over Castlebay
Betoken Barra's Hebridean isle.

W. Blacklaw

MOUNTAIN STREAM

BIRTHED on a mountain,
A wee silver droplet,
Gossamer thread holding me to the hill;
Beginning my journey,
A young, sparkling springlet,
Gaining momentum, alive with the thrill.
Down hillocks, grey-bouldered,
And clothed with pink heather,
I'm rushing and sparkling and leaping
    with glee;
Through valleys, fern-shaded,
In gullies, wherever
My widening curves lead me on to the sea.

Maggie Smith

LARK

A HANDFUL of lark
Buoyant on the strings of
a Summer morning
Twirling and spinning songs
Overtures and symphonies
Though it has learned no music
In the schools of London or Paris
But is sight-reading instead
The kettledrums of the Atlantic
The white bells of the orchids
The violins of the wind.

Kenneth C. Steven

DUSK

THE dusk falls like a curtain
  Upon the fading light,
And draws a veil across the day
As evening turns to night.
The sun is slowly sinking
And in its afterglow
Ghostly moths come out to play
And bats flit to and fro.
There is a sense of quietness
Pervading over all,
And scent of jasmine fills the air
As evening shadows fall.

Kathleen Gillum

PORTRAIT OF SEASONAL GRACE

MICHAELMAS daisy of Autumn,
Glowing in colour today.
Vibrant and rich as the season
To welcome, and brighten our way;
You're part of the floral arrangement
That nature's prepared through the year,
Presenting an intricate pattern
Of beautiful blooms, to appear.
Summer's display is now over,
Autumn now takes pride of place;
Bringing fresh views to enchant us —
— A portrait of seasonal grace . . .

Elizabeth Gozney

GOING HOME

THE morning drums its fingers on the windows
So the glass is left shiny with crying;
Outside the rain feels like thick wool.

There is nothing to separate sea from sky —
Mull has been swallowed in a single gulp,
A ship booms somewhere like a sad whale.

Two small boys scatter puddles with flat feet;
A motorcycle like an insect intent on stinging
Hums by and becomes a thing of the past in mist.

The ferry leaves the island behind a white furl:
Red houses, a jetty, and a huddle of humans —
They are all washed away with the last of the Summer.

Kenneth C. Steven

AUTUMN THE ARTIST

SUCH brilliant gold she splashes on the leaf,
  Such vivid red along the woodland ways,
As if she senses that her time is brief,
Her talent fading with the passing days.

Meantime, she paints the hills in russet hue
And brushes veils of mist across the brae —
Stipples the folded moors in shades of blue
That melt and merge with distance far away.

And then, when shadows spread across the land,
And glowing colours fade as sunbeams die,
Defiantly, she takes her brush in hand
And paints her masterpiece upon the sky!

Brenda G. Macrow

INDIAN SUMMER

WELCOME to our hills and valleys, Indian Summer,
　And to our woods and streams.
You have hushed the songs of the birds
And given us instead a sweet silence,
Telling Winter to wait until you are ready to go.
You have painted the maples in red and gold,
And scattered little white clouds over blue skies.
You are misty mornings and sleepy afternoons
When voices or bells are heard from afar.
Your brown hands rest lightly on the land,
Gentle and kind and comforting.
Indian Summer, you are tranquillity;
Indian Summer, you are love;
Indian Summer, you are the gift of God.

Peter Cliffe

THE REMNANT
OF THE DAY

THE shadows in the evening dusk
  Embrace declining day,
As twilight beckons ghostly bats
And moths to come and play.
The wind is sighing in the trees
As rooks take homeward flight,
And woodsmoke curls from chimney pots
Merging with the night.

One by one the twinkling stars
Peep from a distant place,
Like gems upon a tapestry
Hung out in time and space.
A canopy of tiny lights
Suspended way up high,
Sparkling jewels embroidered on
The curtain of the sky.

The silver sickle of the moon
Gives out an eerie glow,
Streaming down its shining beams
Upon the world below.
The light across the evening sky
Creeps silently away,
As darkness slowly steals upon
The remnant of the day.

Kathleen Gillum

SUMMER'S END

THERE are no leaves now to be seen,
   And all is brown that once was green,
No violet lies in sweet repose,
Nor primrose in the hedgerow grows,
There are no bluebells in the wood,
Bare borders where delphiniums stood,
The cowslips have all disappeared
With columbines and old man's beard,
There is no blossom on the bough,
The air is still and quiet now,
So Mother Nature takes a rest
And holds her children to her breast,
A lullaby she'll softly sing
Until they wake again in Spring.

Brian Hope Gent

AURORA BOREALIS

UP above, all around
A magic lantern show
Of the night sky
Begins
Projecting beams
Of stop light reds
That go on
Forever.
Curtains, purple
And silver green
Fade in
And out
But stick
In our memories
For good.

David Elder

EARLY AFTERNOON

I STOOD upon the river's bank
  To watch bright waters flowing,
And sighed that sweet September day
At thought of Summer going.

The swallows still patrolled above,
A blackbird shrill was calling;
Though every leafy bough was green,
The leaves would soon be falling.

The sky was of the richest blue,
With scarce a white cloud sailing.
Why must I think of drifting snow
And bitter winds loud wailing?

How foolish on a day so fair
To muse on Winter's sorrow!
I tossed a stone, the ripples spread,
And I forgot tomorrow.

Peter Cliffe

AUTUMN MORNING

A LL night the rain sang and played outside;
I heard odd bagpipes of geese
Wandering in circles of lost ghosts overhead.

Now the world has uncurled like a hedgehog
    from sleep —
A blue so clear and sharp —
And the light when it comes is huge.

Breath takes over the whole valley
In the waving of a wand, and the trees
Burst into flames, orange and ochre and gold.

At the door I smell mushrooms and wet fields,
I hear the river's rush
Towards Winter, to the faraway sea.

Kenneth C. Steven

AS EVER NIGHTFALL

LATE September's evening cattle
   Shiver and shuffle along
From one snatched bite to another.

In a gun-metal monocloud sky,
An invisible sun is setting
All over the western hills,

Only the nearest farmhouse
Punctuates the invading dark,
And two inseparable lights

Appear and vanish, appear and vanish,
As they go helter-skelter down,
Dragging a car behind them:

Fine time for the cocked-hat rider
To dismount from the trusty steed
And rap on the coach-house door . . .

For the landlord's finest draught,
The roaring crackling fire
And the rollicking traveller's tale.

Ian Nimmo White

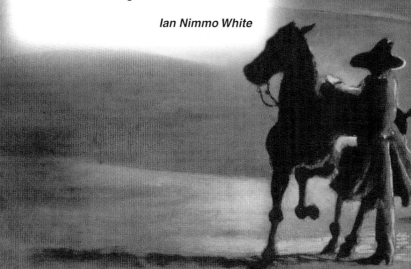

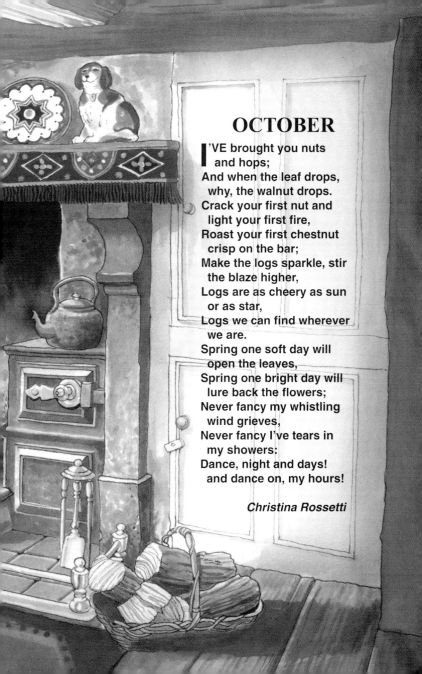

OCTOBER

I'VE brought you nuts
 and hops;
And when the leaf drops,
 why, the walnut drops.
Crack your first nut and
 light your first fire,
Roast your first chestnut
 crisp on the bar;
Make the logs sparkle, stir
 the blaze higher,
Logs are as cheery as sun
 or as star,
Logs we can find wherever
 we are.
Spring one soft day will
 open the leaves,
Spring one bright day will
 lure back the flowers;
Never fancy my whistling
 wind grieves,
Never fancy I've tears in
 my showers:
Dance, night and days!
 and dance on, my hours!

Christina Rossetti

THE HERMITAGE

RESIN incense prickles the nose
in woods fragrant with the sound of water;
Ossian's Hall stands still as a groom
before the sylvan congregation.
As avian choirs practise high above,
pine-cones confetti ground
already strewn with pine needles rice.
Below the nearby bridge,
demure in its veil of moss,
roots dip toes in lace-edged water,
grass skirts tossed high to coyly flash
their garter of fungi.

Rowena M. Love

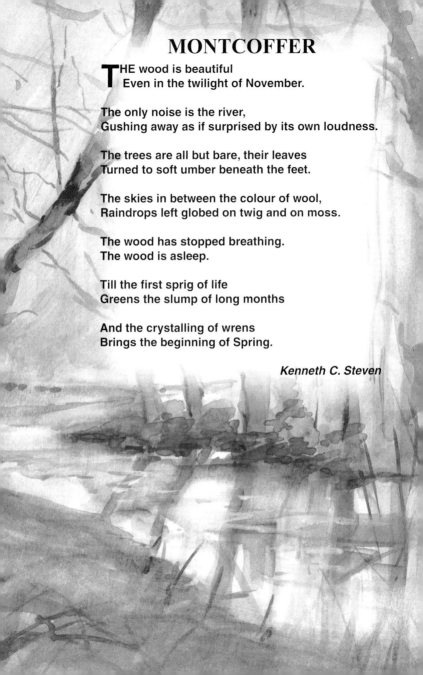

MONTCOFFER

THE wood is beautiful
Even in the twilight of November.

The only noise is the river,
Gushing away as if surprised by its own loudness.

The trees are all but bare, their leaves
Turned to soft umber beneath the feet.

The skies in between the colour of wool,
Raindrops left globed on twig and on moss.

The wood has stopped breathing.
The wood is asleep.

Till the first sprig of life
Greens the slump of long months

And the crystalling of wrens
Brings the beginning of Spring.

Kenneth C. Steven

ESHANESS, SHETLAND

SOLEMN stone dominates
with Gothic extravagance:
vaulted inlets pierced with passages,
crypts hewed by a penitent sea.

Erosion gargoyles cliff edges;
they glare far below
where spray smokes like incense.

Rock is never bare, there, but covered:
by swirls of crushed velvet water;
lichen in a damask weave;
or the congregation of gannets
whose Gregorian chants fill the air.

In the distance, are pulpit stacks
and Eshaness lighthouse, waiting for night,
its unlit candle stark
against stained glass sky.

Rowena M. Love

WHERE SLEEP THE ISLANDS

WHERE Islands sleep on ocean's time
   Blue-green seas swirl, white breakers climb,
And dreamer dreams o'er mist-clad hills
To cloud-capped heaven, where thoughts are still.
I, wand'ring, stray down golden beams
Thro' loch and lea midst murm'ring streams.

O let me sleep where islands dream,
Where oceans sweep like rushing stream,
And sea-spumed sands caress machair,
Soft rustling bow in rhythmic bar,
When splendoured sunset spans the sky,
Brushed tints of gold, red-purple vie.

Thus will I know where Islands sleep,
Where ocean tides their vigil keep.

Frank Stewart

NOVEMBER MORNING

A SQUIRREL rattles undergrowth
then shoots upward,
its mercury rising swifter
than the frost had fallen
to coil fossils in each patch of water.

There's a hole in the sky
where a crow flies:
satin punctured with jagged dark
that frays further with every swoop;
blackbirds crack the brittle silence.

A cabochon ruby gleams in the hedge:
the robin pulsing with life
among leaves' rigor mortis;
sun transforms their sugar coating
to a slow drip of syrup.

Muck's sweet stench fertilises the air;
into the ear of the dying year
it whispers of growth.
Winter will keep its secret safe
until loud-mouthed Spring
spreads it like gossip.

Rowena M. Love

"CASTLES" AND "KINGS"

ON railway station platforms now
   I miss the stench of smoke and steam.
I let the diesel monsters pass,
And much prefer to doze and dream

Of when the "Castles" and the "Kings"
Charged fiercely in with regal pride,
And passengers who stepped on board
Experienced a majestic ride.

These locomotives hauling trains —
Expresses known to me as "crack" —
Like knights in armour thundered by,
Romantic heroes of the track!

"Caerphilly Castle", "King George V" —
The names retain their glamour still,
For they enhanced my tender years
With magic and a special thrill.

Like haunting ghosts, grey wreaths of smoke
Signalled the passing of each train:
A moving, once-familiar sight
Nostalgia brings to life again.

And I relive the days of steam
With engines flashing down the line.
Such spectacles will never fade
While boyhood memories brightly shine.

Glynfab John

THE SEA GYPSY

I AM fevered with the sunset,
I am fretful with the bay,
For the wander-thirst is on me
And my soul is in Cathay.

There's a schooner in the offing,
With her topsails shot with fire,
And my heart has gone aboard her
For the Islands of Desire.

I must forth again tomorrow!
With the sunset I must be
Hull down on the trail of rapture
In the wonder of the sea.

Richard Hovey

TROON BEACH IN SNOW

COLLIE-COLOURED with snow and seaweed,
the beach plays fetch with the Winter crowd.
Snowy hackles raised by last night's frost,
children tug the fur to snowballs,
or smooth it with their sledge,
parents always close at heel.
Teenagers romp in puppy games,
throwing themselves like sticks
through a ruff of waves,
their flesh driftwood-pale against a litmus sky,
where the heavens blend to sunset.

Rowena M. Love

SLEIGHRIDE

A PHANTOM in white wonderland,
   And all-embracing chill,
Diamonds sparkling in the snow,
To strains of nature's quill.
The splendour of this season,
Its special magic stirs,
Red-bibbed little robins,
Midst the oak and conifers.
Frozen fields are muffled,
Sleighs are on the ice,
Brilliance achieving,
With the throw of Winter's dice.

Dorothy McGregor

The artists are:—

Matt Bain; The Remnant Of The Day.
Sheila Carmichael; Butterfly,
Coffee Morning, A Friend's Garden,
Summer's End.
Jackie Cartwright; January Contrast,
River Dee.
John Dugan; Iona, Harlequin And
Columbine, My Lovely Jenny, The
Hermitage, Where Sleep The Islands.
Alan Haldane; Seascape (Borgh Beach,
Barra), Autumn Morning.
Eunice Harvey; Nature's Colours,
Nightly Nocturnes, Autumn The Artist.
Ashley Jennings; The Harbour,
Aurora Borealis.
Harry McGregor; Snowdrops,
Mountain Stream.
Ian McIntosh; Peaceful Waters,
Long-Tailed Tits, Malvern.
Norma Maclean; Snow, Sandstone
Splendour, The Grasshopper And
The Cricket, Going Home, Montcoffer,
Troon Beach In Snow.
Sandy Milligan; Laurencekirk, Lark,
Dusk, November Morning.
Keith Robson; Winter Sonnet,
Hometown, Evening, My Friendly Hill,
Indian Summer, As Ever Nightfall,
October.
David Sharp; Eshaness, Shetland.
Joseph Watson; Lilies Of The Valley,
Early Afternoon.
Staff Artists; Then, Days Of Sunshine,
Wonders, Portrait Of Seasonal Grace,
"Castles" And "Kings", The Sea Gypsy,
Sleighride.

JULY

S	M	T	W	T	F	S
				1	2	3
4	5	6	7	8	9	10
11	12	13	14	15	16	17
18	19	20	21	22	23	24
25	26	27	28	29	30	31

AUGUST

S	M	T	W	T	F	S
1	2	3	4	5	6	7
8	9	10	11	12	13	14
15	16	17	18	19	20	21
22	23	24	25	26	27	28
29	30	31				

SEPTEMBER

S	M	T	W	T	F	S
			1	2	3	4
5	6	7	8	9	10	11
12	13	14	15	16	17	18
19	20	21	22	23	24	25
26	27	28	29	30		